Counting Books

More or Less

A Rain Forest Counting Book

by Rebecca Fjelland Davis

Reading Consultant: Gail Saunders-Smith, PhD

Capstone

Mankato, Minnesota

A+ Books are published by Capstone Press,
151 Good Counsel Drive, P.O. Box 669, Mankato, Minnesota 56002.
www.capstonepress.com

1 2 3 4 5 6 11 10 09 08 07 06

Library of Congress Cataloging-in-Publication Data
Davis, Rebecca Fjelland.
    More or less: a rain forest counting book / by Rebecca Fjelland Davis.
    p. cm.—(A+ books. Counting books)
    Summary: "Simple text and color photos introduce plants and animals found in the rain forest
while explaining basic concepts of addition and subtraction"—Provided by publisher.
    Includes bibliographical references and index.
    ISBN-13: 978-0-7368-6376-6 (hardcover)
    ISBN-10: 0-7368-6376-1 (hardcover)
    1. Counting—Juvenile literature. 2. Arithmetic—Juvenile literature. 3. Rain forest
animals—Juvenile literature. 4. Rain forest—Juvenile literature. I. Title. II. Series.
QA113.D386 2007
513.2'11—dc22   2006007560

Credits

Jenny Marks, editor; Kia Adams, designer; Kelly Garvin, photo researcher/photo editor

Photo Credits

Brand X Pictures, cover (swallowtail butterfly), 20–21 (all)
Digital Vision, back cover (frog), 15, 28
Minden Pictures/Frans Lanting, 4, 7, 16, 17; Konrad Wothe, cover (toucan);
    Mark Moffett, 6; Michael & Patricia Fogden, 5; ZSSD, 14
Nature Picture Library/Anup Shan, 8 (all)
Pete Carmichael, 10, 11, 12, 13 (all), 18, 19, 22–23 (all)
Peter Arnold/Klein, 24–25; R. Andrew Odum, 26–27; WWI/Ted Mead, 2–3
Shutterstock/John Arnold, 29; Mike Von Bergen, back cover (capybara)
Visuals Unlimited/Larry Kimball, 9

Note to Parents, Teachers, and Librarians

More or Less: A Rain Forest Counting Book uses color photographs and a
nonfiction format to introduce children to life in the rain forest while building
mastery of basic counting skills. It is designed to be read aloud to a pre-reader
or to be read independently by an early reader. The images help early readers
and listeners understand the text and concepts discussed. The book encourages
further learning by including the following sections: Facts about Rain Forests,
Glossary, Read More, Internet Sites, and Index. Early readers may need
assistance using these features.

Rain forests are hot, steamy places packed full of life. Let's count rain forest plants and animals.

Two lemurs cling to trees. Their noses sniff to tell if other lemurs have rested in the same tree.

Nearby, one butterfly sips nectar. Which is more, two lemurs or one butterfly?

Two is more than one.

One tree snake slithers over rain forest leaves. It flattens its colorful body to glide from tree to tree.

Three capybaras listen for danger. How many more capybaras than snakes?

Two more!

Two orangutans live high in the trees. They grip branches with their hands and their feet.

One sloth climbs slowly up a branch. Two orangutans plus one sloth equals three tree climbers.

2+2=4

Two green weevils munch on a branch. Weevils will eat almost any kind of plant.

Two shield bugs scamper along
the forest floor. Two weevils plus
two shield bugs equals four bugs.

2+3=5

Two hourglass tree frogs are the size of a quarter. But they make a big noise when they call out to one another.

Three masked puddle frogs join in the singing. Two plus three equals five noisy frogs.

13

Two bearded pigs have very strong snouts. They use their snouts to dig for worms and roots.

One toucan opens its big, colorful bill. Which is less, two bearded pigs or one toucan?

One is less than two.

Five macaws perch on a branch.
Macaws have strong beaks to crack
the hard shells of nuts they eat.

Near the forest floor, two orchids bloom in the tropical heat. Two orchids are how many less than five macaws?

Three less!

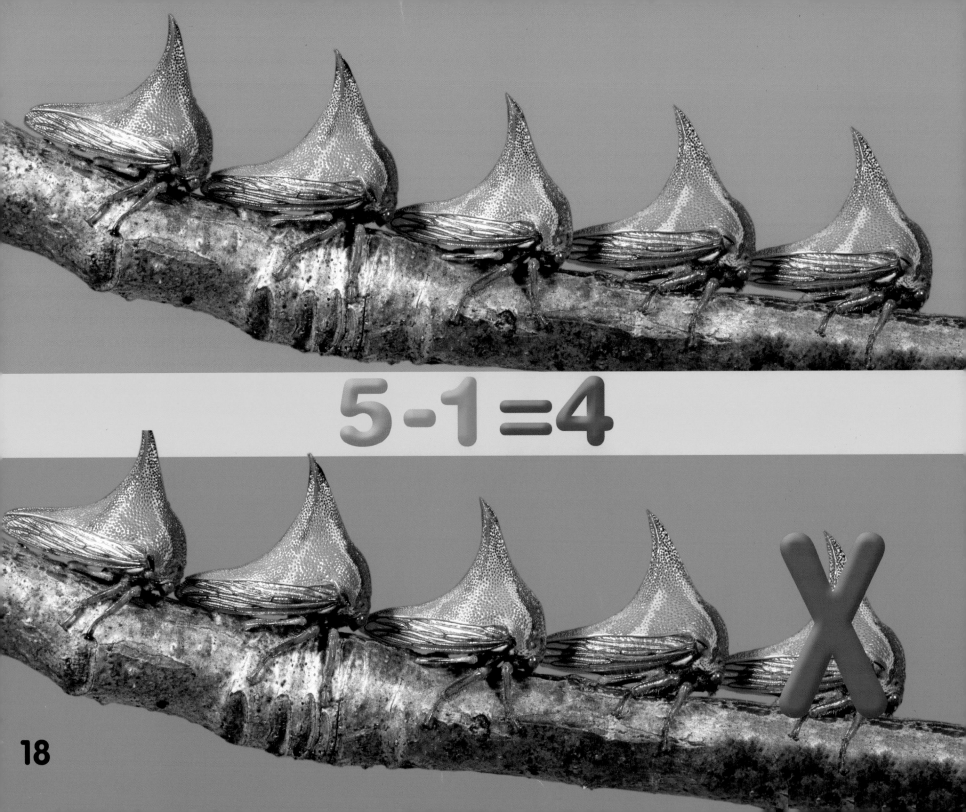

5-1=4

Five thorn bugs minus
one thorn bug equals
four thorn bugs.

5-2=3

Five butterflies minus
two butterflies equals
three butterflies.

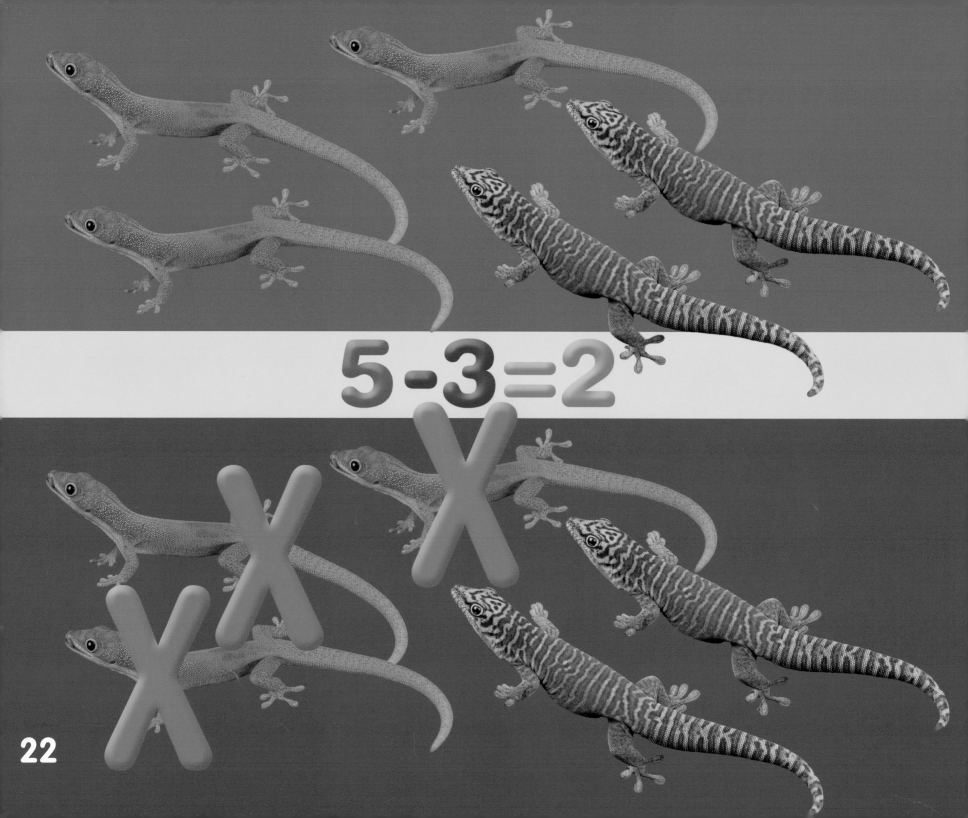

5-3=2

Five geckos minus
three geckos equals
two geckos.

One lone jaguar creeps low looking for food. The other animals hide. One jaguar plus zero animals equals one.

25

5-0=5

Five red-eyed tree frogs watch for a cricket or a moth. Not one frog budges until it catches an insect. Five minus zero equals five.

Facts about Rain Forests

The rain forest is home to more than half of the world's animals.

Thorn bugs look like thorns on a branch. These bugs are actually sharp, and they taste bitter to any bird that dares to eat them.

Macaws are famous for their bright colors. Their feathers of bold red, blue, and yellow actually help them hide in the rain forest. The macaw's coloring helps it to blend in with leaves, fruits, and shadows in the rain forest.

If a capybara hears danger coming, it dives into the water to hide. Capybaras swim and dive very well.

When a toucan sleeps, it rests its large beak on its back. Then it folds its tail up over its head. A sleeping toucan looks like a ball of feathers.

Orchids grow well in rain forests. These flowers need lots of moisture and attract all kinds of rain forest bugs.

Poison dart frogs get their name from a tribe of people in the Colombian rain forest. They catch the frogs with leaves and then dip their blow darts into the frog poison to use for hunting.

Glossary

bearded pig (BIHRD-uhd PIG)—a type of pig with yellowish whiskers on the sides of its long face

capybara (kah-pee-BAIR-uh)—a pig-sized tailless rodent with partly webbed feet

green weevil (GREEN WEE-vuhl)—a type of beetle with a shiny greenish-bronze body

lemur (LEE-muhr)—an animal with large eyes and a long furry tail; lemurs are related to monkeys.

puddle frog (PUHD-uhl FROG)—a type of frog that prefers to live in small pools of water

sloth (SLAWTH)—an animal with long arms and legs, curved claws, and a shaggy coat; sloths move very slowly and hang upside down in trees.

tree frog (TREE FROG)—a small frog that lives in trees; tree frogs have sticky pads on their feet to cling to leaves and branches.

Read More

Galko, Francine. *Rainforest Animals.* Animals in Their Habitats. Chicago: Heinemann, 2003.

Lindeen, Carol K. *Life in a Rain Forest.* Living in a Biome. Mankato, Minn.: Capstone Press, 2004.

Murphy, Stuart J. *More or Less.* MathStart. New York: HarperCollins Publishers, 2005.

Townsend, Dana E. *Day and Night in the Rain Forest.* Get Real Books. Columbus, Ohio: Zaner-Bloser, 2004.

Internet Sites

FactHound offers a safe, fun way to find Internet sites related to this book. All of the sites on FactHound have been researched by our staff.

Here's how:

1. Visit *www.facthound.com*

2. Choose your grade level.

3. Type in this book ID **0736863761** for age-appropriate sites. You may also browse subjects by clicking on letters, or by clicking on pictures and words.

4. Click on the **Fetch It** button.

FactHound will fetch the best sites for you!

31

Index

LISLE LIBRARY DISTRICT

LISLE, ILLINOIS 60532

TEL: (630) 971-1675